A Fancy Jacket

by David Nguyen
illustrated by Susan Lexa

Core Decodable 76

McGraw Hill Education

Bothell, WA • Chicago, IL • Columbus, OH • New York, NY

MHEonline.com

Send all inquiries to:
McGraw-Hill Education
8787 Orion Place
Columbus, OH 43240

ISBN: 978-0-02-144853-1
MHID: 0-02-144853-1

Printed in the United States of America.

8 9 10 LCR 25 24 23

Nancy's fancy jacket was thin.
She could feel the winter chill.

Nancy wished she could run.
But the sidewalk was icy.
She could fall.

Mom looked at Nancy.

She could tell Nancy was freezing.

Mom hugged Nancy.
"That fancy jacket is thin," Mom said.

Nancy's teeth chattered.

"Yes, it is lacy," said Nancy.

"It isn't for winter."

Mom made hot, spicy tea.
"I feel better," said Nancy.
"Hot, spicy tea is for winter."